Legal Stuff We Have to Include:

ISBN 13: 978-0-615-42960-1

ISBN 10: 0615429602

Disclaimer:
The publisher, author, and copyright holder (the collective "we") have put our best efforts into preparing this book, but other than our best efforts, we make NO representation of warranties with respect to this book. *The Freedom Guide for Music Creators* is not rendering legal, accounting, or other professional advice; for legal or other expert assistance, you should seek the services of a suitable professional. We do not guarantee or warrant that the information and opinions in this book will produce any particular results, and we caution readers that the advice and strategies contained in this book may not be suitable for every individual or business. We shall not be liable for any monetary loss, physical injury, property damage, loss of profit or any other commercial damages, including but not limited to special, incidental, consequential, or other damages.

Table of Contents

Introduction

Welcome to the *Freedom Guide for Music Creators*!

Please Fit Your Thinking Cap Securely

I'm going to assume that those of you who are reading this do not take your sole purposes in the music field as making a few gazillion dollars or becoming the next big star – OR that those are your purposes, but that you're curious and practical enough to learn about other aspects of being a musician.

It's good that you take your craft seriously, because to make best use of *The Freedom Guide*, you'll need to put your thinking cap on and fit it very well. We're going to discuss fundamentals of the music business, along with strategies and resources you will not hear about in many books and in much of your musical education.

You might also want to prepare to part with some long-held notions about money, work, economics, and United States history, because this is going to be a no-holds barred look at the world in which you are creating and re-creating music, and at the forces that define this world.

But first, let's get down to terminology. No matter what you do as a musician from here on, I want you to think of yourself as a MUSIC CREATOR or RE-CREATOR. Musicians are essential in the creation, re-creation, and communication of music, a process that predates corporate control and standards by thousands of years.

Once you begin to think of yourself as an essential part of this millennia-old creative process, your perspective may shift. Perhaps you are struggling through private music lessons, or through high school, college, university, or conservatory. Perhaps you are holding down a "day job" to support you while you make your music. You might be an educator, a parent, a grandparent, or other family member; you might be deeply concerned about passing on not only a musical legacy to the coming generations, but also the skills to expand and protect that legacy. I believe the creation of music is essential to the survival of the human race, and that Creation has been stocked with everything you need to fulfill your role. You just have to find and use the storehouses.

This book, I humbly submit, is one of the storehouses prepared for you as you go about your mission. Once you grasp the information presented here and look into the resources you'll learn about at the same time, you will have a knowledge base many, many musicians would love to have BEFORE they get into sad situations such as:

- Having music, profits, and proceeds stolen from them by record companies, fellow songwriters, and sometimes well-meaning people from their school, church, and favorite social networking site.
- Getting humiliated (and sued) on an album release for not getting proper permissions from copyright owners.
- Losing friendships and big money because nobody can agree or prove who wrote what part of a hot hit.

After we have covered the nuts and bolts of making, sharing and protecting music, we are going to talk about music opportunities, strategies, and money that is available to you, along with some ideas that may help you get that money.

We'll also talk about the nature of money, and why the nature of money makes you, the MUSIC CREATOR and/or RE-CREATOR, potentially as powerful as kings of old and the masters of capitalism of the Information Age. And you'll also learn why the same nature of money makes you as vulnerable a victim to corporate masters today as enslaved Africans were to some of the earliest corporate masters. And you'll also learn why "sharecropping," a little-referenced part of the history of the descendents of Africans in America, bears an unfortunate correlation to the problems you may expect when you sign your first contract with the big companies of the music world.

You see why you need that thinking cap?

How to Use This Book

Think of this book as ten short courses of general information on the music business, ten courses that build upon each other. If you take the time to think about, explore, and use some of the information presented in each chapter before moving on to the next chapter, you will get the most possible benefit from *The Freedom Guide*. Feel free to stop at any time to call one of the phone numbers, check one of the Web links, or go find one of the books referenced in this work; this will allow you to gain more information specific to your needs, while also deepening the general knowledge you will gain from this book. *The Freedom Guide* should be the beginning of your journey of learning, a journey that begins right now.

Chapter 1: Copyright, the Bedrock of the Music Business

Copyright. A simple term composed of two words – *copy* and *right* – upon which many musical careers hang. Proper stewardship of your copyrights and proper use of others' copyrights might make you a millionaire. Improper stewardship and use could bankrupt you.

Copyright means *the right to make and distribute copies,* and this extends to works of music, literature, and visual art, and combinations of the same. The minute you get that music, poem, story, or image out of your head and into a tangible form, you have not only created a work of art but an *intellectual property.* Such a property is as real and potentially as valuable as any piece of physical property that you own.

Intellectual Properties Are Everywhere

Think of the physical properties that began as people's ideas!

The printing press was invented only a few hundred years ago – and some millennia ago, somebody was sitting in Egypt along the Nile River and thinking, "I wonder if those *papyri* reeds could be made into something to write on." Also the keyboard, monitor, CPU, chair, lamp, and various kinds of electrical transmitting equipment, at one time were ideas in someone's mind.

While we are not all equal in terms of our physical possessions, everybody has the opportunity to create and own their own intellectual properties. Today when somebody invents a new product or system, the ideas involved are considered as intellectual properties known as *patents.* When somebody writes a new song, the ideas involved are considered as intellectual properties known as copyrights. The tangible items of music -- sheet music and various types of recordings – would not exist but for the ideas that musicians create. Copyrights are *the bedrock of, and the most valuable thing in, the music business*, at least in terms of generating income.

Sheet music, albums, and videos have a definite price. But copyrights can generate millions of recordings and millions of dollars; the only limit to a copyright's value is the musical skill and business knowledge of those that possess and use it.

Peter M. Thall in his *What They'll Never Tell You About the Music Business* gives an example of the value of copyright that is very important in these troubled economic times. Many people know the name of Irving Berlin, who gave us "God Bless America," "Blue Skies," "Steppin' Out with My Baby," and other songs still popular today. Mr. Berlin was very prolific in the late 1920s and through the 1930s, and Mr. Thall tells you why: Mr. Berlin's only means of keeping himself and his family fed during the Great Depression was his royalties from his copyrights. The value of Mr. Berlin's copyrights was literally the difference between feeding himself and his family, or not – quite possibly between life, and death.

The Great Dividing Line of the Music Business

The musical world is largely divided between those that understand and leverage the value of copyright and those who do not.

A similar line divides corporate owners, whose corporations are based upon a set of patents, copyrights, and *trademarks* (the intellectual property term for brand names and logos), from their workers. Workers may reproduce and transport a company's intellectual properties in tangible form, but many workers are not allowed to gain ownership in the physical products or the ideas behind them.

Many publishing and record executives would love to get you into the position of the average worker. Many of them would love to have you build their nest of intellectual property by signing what you create over to them, and they would love to have you running around to sell the physical items they will then own – the albums, the videos, the music books – for a bit of cash. I say a bit of cash because of the billions of dollars that are made and lost in the music industry every year. But you now know what the music executives and corporate owners know about the great dividing line between you and them. Much of the rest of *The Freedom Guide* will help you leverage that knowledge to your advantage.

Protecting Your Copyright

When you have written down your song or recorded it for the first time, you have created an *exclusive* bundle of rights slapped under the general title copyright. These rights are laid out in the United States Copyright Law and include:

- The right to make copies, in visual or audio form
- The right to distribute copies, through sheet music, through recordings, through digital transmissions (think Mp3s and the like)
- The right to publish through mass distribution and public performances

Generally speaking (there are exceptions for educational, scholarly, and religious uses), *no one* has the right to make, distribute, or publish your works without your express permission.

This doesn't mean, however, that other people won't press their luck.

Theft is huge in the world of intellectual property, and theft of the rights inherent in music is perhaps the easiest and possibly the most devastating. All someone has to do – and your associates and co-writers are more likely suspects than the stranger who hears your song while passing by your window – is record a performance of your song or steal your sheet music and put a different name on it. It happens every day to composers who haven't read the next paragraph:

To protect your work from theft, promptly register your copyrights with the appropriate government agency in your country of origin. Appendix B has the contact and relevant information for selected international copyright offices and links to every copyright office in the world – you're covered, wherever you are. We'll deal with the United States here, but the principles are similar just about everywhere.

In the United States, the Copyright Office of the Library of Congress handles these affairs. Here is the address and phone number:

U.S. Copyright Office
101 Independence Avenue SE
Washington, DC 20559-6000
(202) 707-3000

You can send for a wealth of further information about copyright and how to protect it. Or you can go to the Web site, at http://www.copyright.gov. Go to the "About Copyright" section.

The Copyright Office has recently changed its registration methods, simplifying them and gearing them much more toward computer users. The Office would prefer you to register your works online through its Electronic Copyright Office. Pay by debit or credit card, and upload a computer file of your work. The cost for this is $35, plus $1 for each additional title submitted if you are registering works as a group. You can also apply to pre-register your works before they are finished, but that's $115 – and the fee is non-refundable no matter what the Office decides about your pre-registration.

You can register your works with form CO, which is a type-in PDF form (you'll need Adobe Acrobat Reader to open the file). You fill in the blanks, print the file out, and send it along with your sheet music or recording and a check for $50. Add $3 for each additional title if registering a group of works. Form CO is what I use and recommend to my clients, by the way, although my curiosity about the Electronic Copyright Office is growing. But I like to have that form to print out and file, and for that, nothing beats Form CO.

Paper forms are still available by request; you'll need to ask for form PA for sheet music, and form SR for sound recordings, and this costs $65.

A Little Extra Something For Internet Protection

If you intend to put out a great deal of your work online from anywhere in the world, standard copyright registration is a definite place to start, but you might want to do more.

The great thing about the Internet is that it is just about everywhere at once, instantly – the bad thing about the Internet is that anything you put out on it is out there instantly, irretrievably, and *forever*. Even if you don't have a single fan, some computer or server somewhere will have a copy of your work sitting on it – and the more times your song is transmitted and downloaded, the more servers and computers will retain a copy. And servers are linked around the world. Your song can travel farther and faster on the Internet than you ever intended, far enough and fast enough to strain the limits of standard copyright protection.

To find a way to use the qualities of the Internet to your advantage in protecting your songs, you might consider registering a copy of your works with the Worldwide Online Creators' Registry, which you'll find at http://www.worldwideocr.com/Copyright_songs.asp.

The main use of copyright registration is to prove *when* you wrote a particular work, for legal purposes. The Registry applies an online registration with an encrypted file that contains the dates and distinguishing characteristics. The file can only be unlocked by you. Also, the Registry provides you a virtual safe deposit box where you can keep digital files of all your works (provided they are smaller than 20 megabytes).

There are several membership options for the Registry, ranging from $20 for one year's access to $99 for five years' access. Renewal rates range from $10 for each additional year to $35 for new five-year periods. Each of the options for original membership comes with credits you can use toward registration of your work; the $20 one-year plan comes with seven credits; the five-year $99 plan comes with 50 credits. After you have exhausted your credits, you may register individual works for $3 (and sometimes less) and whole albums (up to 20 songs, in Mp3 format, of course) for $59.

One word of caution – the Registry is not quite a replacement for the various copyright offices around the world, simply because your safe deposit box and your registrations only last for as long as you maintain your membership. If you let your membership expire with the Registry, your protections expire as well. That is the great danger. Your copyright lasts for decades after your death – not only will you have to maintain lifelong vigilance (and payments to the Registry), but your children and perhaps your grandchildren will be on the hook as well. By contrast, the Copyright Office charges you once and no further maintenance or fees are necessary.

On the other hand, the useful life of a copyright is usually a lot shorter than its actual life. Even if you write an absolute smash hit, much of your money will be made within the first decade or two after it becomes a hit.

Some pieces of music do become so popular that they produce income year after year for the entire life of the copyright, and beyond. If Beethoven could come back, complete his tenth symphony, get married, have some kids, and live another 40 years from today, his family would be sitting pretty on royalties well into the 22nd Century, just based on Beethoven's past successes.

Or, taking a more recent example, I heard Duke Ellington's "Very Special" on *CSI* the other night. Even though Mr. Ellington passed away in 1974, the owners of his copyrights are likely to receive a nice amount of royalties until the middle of this century, and his music will be making money for somebody long after that.

But such cases are rare. Most copyrights only need protection over their useful life. So, if you have many, many pieces of music that you need to register, you estimate the useful life of these works will be 5-20 years, and you intend to distribute most of your music online, the Registry can be a cost-effective and useful tool. But consider its usage carefully.

What Your Protections Can Do For You

No matter what method you choose (if you have a hit, you might want both) your registration is your proof of ownership, good in courts of law across most of the world. If someone steals your work, you can shut down their theft posthaste. According to the United States Copyright Law, your remedies include even having illegal copies destroyed.

Or, just wait. If the offender makes millions of dollars, you can wait and then sue for the millions with an excellent chance of success. But be warned: if you give people the impression that you're quick to sue, these same people will be nervous about using your music in the future. And, many cases of improper use of music are not meant maliciously. Many people don't know you can't do anything you want with somebody else's music. We'll talk about that more in Chapter 2 – but the point is that you don't want to handle these cases with too heavy a hand.

Here's what I would do – and I owe the first part of this strategy to Eric Beall, author of *Making Music Make Money.* Find the best lawyer you can to write a letter informing the offender of their infringement on your rights, and offer to settle out of court – that is, you offer the infringer the opportunity to stop the infringement and pass the money they've made across to you, without the hassle (for you) and embarrassment (for the infringer) of a trial.

In the case in which an *accidental* infringer made absolute millions off your work, you don't have to leave them anything, but I – not Mr. Beall in this case – would leave that person maybe 5 percent. The infringer in that case would have done something for you few publishers and record companies could ever do – get your music worldwide exposure and create streams of income for you that could last for decades. I'd say losing 95 percent of the results of all that work is more than sufficient punishment; the 5 percent is something of an acknowledgement of the work said person has put in. Or, you might even hire that person; after all, look how rich the person has made you!

One More Thing . . .

I am about to do you a big, BIG favor, and alert you to what I have discovered is the No. 1 problem when it comes to copyright drama: Your co-writers can be the most likely small-time suspects (more about the "big-time" folks you need to watch out for later).

Say you sit down with a few associates and write a song with him or her – no big deal, just a fun way to spend an afternoon. The fun continues as you and your co-writers begin showing off the song to your friends. The fun may turn into a party if your friends and their friends become a small and enthusiastic audience that just keeps growing and growing and growing . . .

Yet I guarantee you the party will be over for you if the song becomes a hit and big money comes to call before you and your co-writers agree on what percentage of the song each individual owns. Unless you and your co-writers are a particularly saintly group of people, I can guarantee that at least some of the individuals you wrote the song with suddenly will be focused on how much of the coming money they can get from the song – and suddenly, whatever part they wrote in the song will become, in their eyes, worth the lion's share of the profits. This is the point at which friendships end, groups break up, and, every now and again, if the money is big enough, somebody gets physically hurt or killed.

But, there are less dramatic but still devastating ways that these things play out, as I have learned from the experience of having songwriters cry on my shoulder. To make it very simple, if you don't get who is responsible for what part of a song sorted out, the copyright laws can't help you. According to the law of the United States, part owners of a copyright are treated the same as full owners. If you have two co-writers, each one of them has as much right as you do to register the copyright of the song, make publishing and recording deals, and enter into binding contracts regarding the song -- and without consulting you first. A co-writer evil enough and shrewd enough will not give you the opportunity for drama; he or she will simply go register the copyright, sign the contracts, and walk off with the song and all the profits when he or she is good and ready. And again, if you don't bother to get the ownership issues in a co-written song sorted out before trouble starts, the legal system usually can't help you – it cannot do for you what you have failed to do for yourself.

So, don't fail – whenever you co-write a song, sit down with everybody involved and write a split letter. A split letter is nothing fancy – just put the date on the page, get everybody to agree and sign to what percentage of the song each individual owns before or just after the song's creation, make copies for everyone (a trip to a notary might not be a bad idea if you know there's a good chance the song could become even slightly profitable), and file your copy where you can get it. If you are the co-writer of a song that is already being performed but is not yet making much money, go to your co-writers before money lust hits and say, "Gee, folks, this song may really take off – we'd better be sure that we each know what we have coming to us. I have this split letter here just to make sure we're all protected . . . ."

If at the beginning of the song process a co-writer refuses to sign a split letter, *do not write a song with that person.* If later on, when the song is finished and out in the world, and a co-writer refuses to sign a split letter, do not waste time on drama. Go to the nearest computer or telephone and get access to whatever copyright registration medium you prefer, fill out the form with your names and the names of all the other co-writers, and register a copy of the song (sheet music or recording) as soon as possible. You will not be able to stop a co-writer from entering contracts and deals without your knowledge, but if big money starts to roll in and your copyright registration is the only one or the first on record, the courts may be able to help you get *some* of the profits you deserve, maybe enough to at least cover your legal fees.

It all starts, no matter your situation, in getting that copyright registration. So, take a break from *The Freedom Guide* and get what you need to protect your work.

Chapter 2: The Flip (and Dangerous) Side of Copyright

Please pay careful attention: if you want to use other people's work, you need to get permission. If you want to record or arrange or excerpt somebody else's song – or even make photocopies in many cases – you need to get permission from the composer or the composer's publisher.

Make no mistake: one high-profile case of infringement, intentional or not, will severely damage your musical career. Infringement could also clear out your bank account. According to the United States Copyright Law, each case of willful infringement can cost you $100,000. Unintentional use can cost you from $400 to $10,000. So don't take chances – do not use other people's works without the proper permissions!

Fortunately, permissions are not all that hard to get. After all, composers and publishers want you to use their works. Here's how you can get the permissions you need:

- If you are doing an album with somebody else's works, you'll need a *mechanical license* from the composer or publisher. Apply to the copyright holders directly. The present rate is 9.1 cents per song.
- If you need to photocopy sheet music or make overheads for a song, you'll need a *miscellaneous license*; again, apply directly.
- If you're looking for songs for church services, Copyright Licensing International offers a Church Copyright License for more than 150,000 songs. Call them at 1-800-234-2446 or go to www.ccli.com.
- If you are doing a live performance, the venue where you are performing will be responsible for getting the proper permissions. But, if you're performing out of your home or place of business, you'll need to get a license from the composer or publisher's performing rights organization

(commonly called PROs). Call and ask publishers and composers what PRO they work with on specific songs. In the United States, the PROs are ASCAP (1-800-952-7227 and www.ascap.com), BMI (212-586-2000 and www.bmi.com), and SESAC (615-320-0055 and www.sesac.com).

If you are a composer/arranger, apply to publishers or composers directly for permission to either arrange or include parts of their work in your work.

When you apply to companies or composers, they will send out a simple contract defining your usage of the song, and a credit line to place on your sheet music or CD or liner notes (paper-based or digital). Generally they will send two copies of the contract, one for you to sign and keep, one for you to send back to them. You will either send a check for the required royalties with the contract or you will prepay the amount online, depending on the company.

When getting permissions, *start early*. Composers and publishing companies are not obligated to go along with your schedule, so think ahead about the permissions you'll need and get them as soon as possible.

Or, Call In Some Help . . .

The other way to handle this is to work with a company that will do the work to get that licensing search and payment process taken care for you (for a small fee, of course). And, many major publishers have tried to help you in this respect; they have turned their entire licensing process over to the Harry Fox Agency (http://www.harryfox.com). If you are trying to get a mechanical license for a song and the publisher of that song works with Harry Fox, you just pay Harry Fox $15 plus the amount you need for the mechanical licenses (that is, $15 + 9.1 cents per copy of the song you're going to put in your project), and Harry Fox takes care of the rest. Harry Fox offers a nice discount on its fee if you are licensing more than five songs at a time.

But what if the publisher of the song you want to license doesn't work with Harry Fox? Have no fear: Limelight (http://www.songclearance.com) is here! Limelight's musician-designed platform interfaces with 100 percent of the publishing market, and can clear not only mechanical licenses in the context of putting cover songs on physical CDs, but also in terms of publishing royalties for digital, streaming, and ringtone releases. You use Limelight's easy-to-manage platform to give the company information about the song you want and what you plan to do with it; then Limelight's research team takes over to get you what you need. There is a YouTube video that can walk you through the Limelight process, at http://www.youtube.com/songclearance#p/u/1/o4zhdZF7CK0.

On average, Limelight can get a license secured for an artist within 10-15 days. That is a whole lot better than the 11 months I once spent hunting down a license, only to find out it was in the public domain (more about that later)! And, Limelight's fee structure is approximately the same as Harry Fox -- $15 per song, with discounts if you license more than three songs.

What if you're a choir director just trying to put together some practice materials for your choir – what if you just want to make some practice CDs? Again, have no fear; ChoirParts (http://www.choirparts.com) is here! ChoirParts provides fully licensed rehearsal Mp3s (or CDs) for many kinds of choral music -- although much of the calls ChoirParts gets are for today's complex gospel songs, it also handles classical choral pieces as well, including Handel's *Messiah*. ChoirParts provides parts for soprano, alto, tenor, and bass, so that choir members can study their parts at their own convenience. The $25 fee includes the mechanical licensing fees ChoirParts pays to the copyright holders of the songs you want, thereby sparing you the search time. ChoirParts generally turns around parts for songs it works on in seven days.

A heads-up for you savvy choral composers who can't pay a choir to help you do that demo -- why not submit a request to ChoirParts and see what happens? The quality of the company's work would make it more than worth your while to explore the possibility!

An Alternative Source of Usable Works

If you don't care for all these licensing goings-on, there is a solution: use music in the *public domain*. This is music that either is folk music – no particular person holds the copyright – or in which copyright has expired, which in the United States would be any piece of music written and printed before 1923. Now, be careful: things go into the public domain at different rates in different countries. See Appendix B to find international copyright offices that have information on when copyright expires in other countries. The general principles written below, however, apply just about everywhere.

In most cases, you must work from copies of sheet music that bear the original copyright notice. Occasionally, publishers just reprint such music without altering it; no copyright notice is attached in those cases, and as long as you double-check that the piece was composed before 1923, you can use the piece. But if a new arrangement has been made of that piece, the copyright of the arrangement belongs to the arranger and publisher. You will need permission to use that arrangement.

Good sources for public domain music include libraries (online and offline), used music stores, and educational centers. Estate and yard sales can sometimes be rich sources as well. You can also search the Copyright Office at http://www.copyright.gov, the Library of Congress at http://www.loc.gov, and a whole site full of public domain music resources at http://www.pdinfo.com. For public domain classical music, check out The Mutopia Project at http://mutopiaproject.org, the IMSLP / Petrucci Music Library at http://imslp.org/wiki/Main_Page, and ChoralWiki at http://www.cpdl.org. Arrangements you create from public domain music become your new copyrights. For composers and arrangers this is a huge source of fresh ideas. Artists can also make both sides of copyright work for them by working in the public domain.

The public domain does have its own set of rules. You still have to give credit where credit is due, to composers as well as to communities that create folk music, and there are other quirks that will be discussed in the Appendix. But in general, the use of the public domain can ease your difficulties in finding music to use.

So much then for the flip side of copyright – not so dangerous after all, if you stay on the right side of the line when it comes to using other people's music.

BUT WHAT IF YOU'VE ALREADY CROSSED THAT LINE?

What if you have already recorded and/or arranged several of your favorite songs without getting the proper permissions? What if you are selling these songs as an album or online? What if you are doing nothing but ripping songs from your favorite CDs and sending them to your friends across the instant, irretrievable, and *forever* universe of the Internet?

The Freedom Guide is no substitute for good legal advice from a skilled intellectual property lawyer. But, good common sense allows one piece of advice:

IN THE NAMES OF MUSICIANS WHO ARE STRUGGLING TO COLLECT ENOUGH ROYALTIES TO SURVIVE, AND FOR THE SAKE OF JUSTICE, FAIR PLAY, SANITY, AND YOUR FUTURE CAREER AND BANK ACCOUNT, STOP INFRINGING COPYRIGHTS, RIGHT NOW!

Since you have read this chapter, you can't say you don't know about needing copyright permissions – and willful infringement could cost you up to $100,000! So please stop selling any albums of improperly used songs, clean up your Web site, and please don't rip any more songs off of other people's albums!

But What about Sampling?

I recently had the question of meeting with one of the highly intelligent readers of the first edition of this book, who asked me about something I didn't cover in the first edition: Is sampling all right?

My answer: Sampling is wonderful, if you do it right.

Allow me to present an analogy. If you are in a store, and you see samples of perfume or food, you know immediately that the food or perfume is on offer from the store and that it's okay to take a taste or spray some on for free. But, if you start nibbling, spraying, and walking out the door with items that are for sale and not clearly on offer for free, there is another term for what you are doing: shoplifting, also known as stealing.

Like grocery and department store, like record store – or song owned by someone other than you. So far as the law of the United States is concerned, when you take that hot drum riff or tagline out of a song owned by somebody else and make tracks for your song out of it without the copyright owner's permission, you are stealing – you are infringing the copyright of the owner of the song. This has been legally settled since 2004, when the 6th Circuit Court of Appeals ruled that sampling was a copyright infringement on the same level as stealing the whole song -- license needed, or else! Now, somewhere down the pike, there may be something called a "Compulsory Sampling License," which will set a reasonable, statutory rate of payment for folks that want to use parts of other people's songs. But while waiting for that particular ship to come in, you would be well-advised to NOT take that loop out of whatever hot song you like on the radio, on CD, or on MP3. If the case that went to the 6th Circuit Court proves anything, it proves that even if you change the key, speed, and even sequence of your sample, you will still be in danger the minute you make significant money from the song you built on an "un-cleared" sample.

Okay, I know what you're thinking: "If there's such a thing as an 'un-cleared' sample, there must be a way to get a cleared sample, a way to clear the use of the sample I want." There is, but you're not going to like it. Remember how I said there may be a "Compulsory Sampling License" in the future? The mechanical license I talked about a little bit earlier is a compulsory license. If you ask for a license to cover somebody's song on your new project, the copyright owner is compelled – hence, it is compulsory -- to give it to you based on the rate established by law, a mere 9.1 cents per recording per song. But there is no such compulsion when it comes to clearing samples; you have to negotiate directly with whoever owns the song you are sampling. And, since often a sample loop makes up a lot of the music of a song – and was sampled because it had just that catchy beat or riff – the owner of a song may demand a very hefty fee. I've heard of cases in which the price of clearing a sample cost anywhere from 50 percent to ALL of a song's royalties.

Notice I am not saying, "Do not sample." I am saying, don't do it the way most people do it. I am saying, go listen to LOCAL artists and approach them as you would approach a co-writer – let them know what you like about their songs, what you'd like to do with a sample of their work, and where you see their sample providing value for them as well as for you. Local musicians are like you – they are looking for additional opportunities for exposure, performances, and air play, and would be glad for your help IF you approach them and their work with respect. This way, you create a win-win situation.

Make sure to go back and review what I said in Chapter 1 about handling your co-writing business -- if you sample from a local artist, you'll still need a split letter.   Just as a rough guide: figure out how much of the song, approximately, the sampled and looped material makes up. If it's the only accompaniment to whatever words you have going on, you had better offer 50 percent of the song to the person you're sampling.   But another metric is important; if the sample is used only a few times, but each of those times is in the hook of the song, the part that makes people want to hear the song again and again, you might again consider offering 50 percent of the song to the person you're sampling. I know, I know – presumably, this is the situation we were trying to avoid in clearing a sample in the first place.   But in this case you are gaining a local partner, who will be helping you promote the song you share.

Oh, by the way – and this goes for co-writing too – don't sample from folks who have no hustle, who can't or won't help you. Even if the person you are sampling from has the catchiest beat since Famous Rapper So-and-So laid down THAT track, if that person has no hustle to get the song he or she now owns with you moving in his or her circles, that means you will be doing 100 percent of the work for a lesser percent of the profits. For "no hustle" is always relative. The person that can't be bothered to help you push your shared song today is the same person who will be first to show up with demands when your solitary labors produce the fruit of cash tomorrow. Believe it, dear reader – it is as sure as the sun rising tomorrow.   In the music business, everyone has hustle when it comes to collecting from YOU.   So don't put yourself in that situation – the minute you realize the artist you want to sample from doesn't show any interest in what you're planning to do with their work, make a quick and gracious exit.   Tracks are plentiful. Great tracks are rare. Reliable working partners in the business of music are priceless. Don't sample yourself short.

When you have everything sorted out (or, in the best of all worlds, there will be nothing to sort out), *The Freedom Guide* will be right here, ready to talk about "music money," also known as royalties.

Chapter 3: Royalties

Now that we've discussed copyright, let's talk about royalties, the lifeblood of music creators, re-creators, and rich record and publishing companies everywhere.

Royalties are easiest understood as a form of rent payments. Consider that in the world of physical property, we have something called "real estate." The word *real* is the Spanish word for king, or royal, and at one time across much of Europe, kings and nobles owned all the land. The citizens of the Middle Ages had to work the land in order to stay on it. Even today, your property tax has to be paid to governments, which carry on some functions of the royals of old.

This brings us back to royalties. In the world of intellectual property, copyrights are "real estate," owned by the "royals" otherwise known as composers, songwriters, arrangers, and artists, along with their publishers, record companies, and record labels. People who want to make use of music are required to pay royalties to copyright owners.

Four major kinds of royalties yield cash to music creators and re-creators:

- **Performance Royalties:** These are due whenever a piece of music is performed in public (live or through recordings on TV, radio, and the Internet), with the exception of religious services and certain non-profit and educational uses. Performance rights societies such as ASCAP (www.ascap.com or 1-800-952-7227), BMI (www.bmi.com or (310) 659-9109), or SESAC (www.sesac.com or 615-320-0055) assist musicians in collecting these funds.

- **Mechanical Royalties:** These are due whenever a piece of music is reproduced on cassettes, CDs, DVDs, videos (but there is more to that) and Internet files. The standard royalty rate for 2007 was 9.1

cents, with adjustment upward for longer pieces; new rates are presently being negotiated.

- **Synchronization Royalties:** These are due whenever a piece of music is put into a movie, a television show, a documentary, a podcast, a video game, a TV commercial . . . the possibilities of music being combined with moving images are many. These royalties produce thousands of dollars for many composers.

- **Print Royalties:** This, of course, deals with what happens when sheet music is sold. For many musicians this source of royalties is often seen as being in decline, but it is still quite lucrative, particularly for those that use many instruments in their arrangements.

There are also miscellaneous royalties that are due when a song is used as a ringtone, when its lyrics show up in a piece of literature, and on and on and on. This category is the catch-all for whatever doesn't or hasn't yet been fitted into the other four categories. Much money is made and lost in this category, because even if you don't know to exploit some of the things in here, somebody else does!

Theoretically, one hit song can receive millions of dollars in royalties from all four major categories, and pick up lots of strange things in the miscellaneous department. In other words, one hit song can pull in millions of dollars over a few decades. Brothers Jeffrey and Todd Brabec in their book *Music, Money, and Success* describe more than a dozen sources of royalties a hit song can generate.

Still, you may write a hit song and never see a dime of royalties. Much depends on your contractual relationships with the big companies of the music industry, who are as eager to possess your hard-earned money as you are. Now that you know what you have to defend, and the fundamental steps to start that defense, *The Freedom Guide* is going to tour the battleground with you.

Chapter 4: Why the Record Companies are Rich and You're Not, Part 1

Before you have any kind of contract with the record or publishing companies, have the contract looked over by a lawyer who has understanding and experience with the ins and outs of music law and business. *The Freedom Guide* is not a substitute for good legal advice, but you will learn some things you may need to talk with your lawyer about.

Contracts for artists, artist-songwriters, composers, and arrangers with big companies generally break down in this way; in return for a publisher or record company's access to stores, necessary equipment, studios, distribution outlets, and ability to get music to folks needing music in film, radio, and various other things, music creators or re-creators give administrative control and partial ownership of their copyrights to the company. In this book we will concentrate on the basic forms of contracts, but you might want to pick up Peter M. Thall's *What They'll Never Tell You about the Music Business* for a detailed look at the different types of contracts musicians seek with big companies.

Contracts with publishers consider royalties as having two parts. The "writer's share" of the royalties belongs to the creator of the piece of music, and the "publisher's share" of the royalties belongs to the publisher of the piece of music. The standard split is 50 percent for each party. However, a musician who is willing and able to handle some of the work of shopping their music to record companies, filmmakers, and other venues might sign what is called a *co-publishing* deal. In that case the big company involved takes a smaller share of royalties, perhaps 25 percent.

Eric Beall's *Making Music Make Money* is an excellent text for composers and songwriters considering either co-publishing or *self-publishing,* which describes the work of the musician who publishes his or her own music. Peter Spellman's *The Self-Promoting Musician* is another fine resource. Many of the resources that follow in the remainder of *The Freedom Guide* also are designed to help you take a more active hand in the publication and administration of your music.

The Artist's Dilemma

Artists who are reading this may be thinking, "Wait a minute! Where is the 'artist's share' in all these contracts? After all, we do the work that makes all the money for the record companies, publishers, and music creators – where is our contractual share?" Unfortunately, if you are an artist who does not write or arrange your own music, *there is no share* for you. You have to take whatever the composers, publishers, and record companies will let you have in your record contracts, and unless you are vigilant, you may not get much.

The artist's dilemma is similar to that of employees working for a corporation; while the employees may create much of the revenue and even some of the assets, nothing in the company belongs to the employee. The company belongs to the stockholders and the creditors. Whatever is left over after paying off the creditors and pleasing the stockholders is what the employees get – and if projections say there will be nothing left, employees get laid off.

Similarly, music legally belongs to its creators and to whomever they have assigned their rights to. Whatever companies and composers are willing to give up is the maximum the artist can get. And while an artist cannot be laid off in the traditional sense, some record contracts have surprises far worse.

Must-Haves (And Must-Not-Haves) For Every Record Contract

All musicians, but artists in particular, need to make sure they have an *audit clause* in their contracts with publishers and record companies. An audit clause gives you the right to check your royalty statements (ideally with the help of a lawyer and accountant). Without an audit clause, you will never be able to know for sure if you are due to be paid and how much, but you'll need to be able to follow the money for lots of battles.

Let's start with the advance, or money a publisher or record company may give you up front when you sign a contract. Advances are intended to support you while you do what you do best -- make music. But advances are a loan, and the collateral is all the royalties your music produces in the period covered by the advance. If your music produces enough in royalties to repay the advance, the record company should begin paying you your share of royalties.

But you may never know when those payments should start coming if you don't have an audit clause in your contract. Many companies may not tell you when you have earned enough royalties to be paid. They may give you thousands or even tens of thousands in advances, but be able to keep millions and millions over decades. Why would they disturb a situation like that? You have to be the one to shake things up, and not just about the advances.

If you are an artist, you may have a further problem. United States Copyright Law provides that the owners of copyrights, be they musicians or companies, are to be paid for every record distributed and sold. Producers have also secured the custom of being paid from the first sale. But the artist gets hit with a problem called *recoupment.*

Major record companies and publishers may pass you an advance, but they will not pay you a further dime until they have recouped, that is, made back, every cost of making your album. All pressing, packaging, and promoting your album, every music video, every hour of studio time, every bit of tour support, every expense a record company takes on your behalf will be charged against your royalties. Many albums never break even, and so many artists never get paid.

An audit clause will at least give you the right and the ability to see if your album has broken even. But a better strategy is to get ahead of recoupment problems. The better an idea you have of what support you need from your record label of choice, the less you will be dazzled and confused if your record company starts offering you big shiny things that may or may not help you but that will drain you of royalties in the long run.

Also, try to get something called the *cross-collateralization clause* knocked out of your contract. A cross-collateralization clause provides that if your first album doesn't generate enough royalties to recoup its costs, the company gets to draw recoupment from the second album's royalties for the first album *in addition to the recoupment for the cost of the second album*. And if the costs of the first and second album are not recouped from the royalties of the second album, then it all gets rolled over into the third album, and the fourth album . . .

Another twist in the cross-collateralization horror story: Say you put together some revenue opportunities *separate* from the promotion of your album. Say your album is such a hit that you are offered and can take the opportunity to be the opener for a live concert for some other artist. Or, that same artist asks you to make a guest appearance on their music video. In such a situation you would be generating royalties that have not cost your record company anything, and so that money ought to flow to you directly. These royalties are sometimes referred to as "outside" revenues.

But some versions of the cross-collateralization clause say that unrecouped expenses can be collected from royalties generated by *all* of your royalty producing activities. If you can't get the cross-collateralization clause knocked out entirely, make sure the clause does not contain language that allows your record company to take part of your outside revenues.

Also, try to get a clause put in that makes an exception to packaging charges *on digital distribution*. Some record companies (and publishers as well, with digital sheet music) play a dirty trick: they charge for packaging on digital distribution as if they can transmit a plastic CD cover and album liner through the telephone lines, cable networks, and wireless access points. Now if you don't get the audit clause in, there's little point in arguing about packaging on distribution recoupment, because many companies will not tell you what was distributed digitally and what was distributed physically. But if you can get the audit clause, attack this issue vigorously!

Also, look for the *reserve* clause. Companies will hold a certain percentage of physical albums in reserve as a guard against flooding the market in a time of weak sales. The problem is that the costs of the albums held but not sold – and therefore not producing royalties -- are going to be charged against you just as surely as the records that are selling. Some companies want to hold as much as a third of albums produced on a new release. See if you can amend the reserve clause in your contract to require reserves of no more than 15 percent.

Many record companies want to pay no royalties for records they distribute as free promotional items. And yet these same things will be charged back against artists. Many record companies also want to reduce or eliminate royalties on items they put out at reduced prices (you know, the bargain barrel at your local music store). Try to negotiate a royalty rate floor for such sales, and a similar clause for free distributions.

Special Problems for Songwriters and Artist-Songwriters

Composers and songwriters gain mechanical royalties when they get the songs they have composed or arranged onto an album – if a song is under five minutes, the minimum rate defined by federal statute was 9.1 cents per song in 2007. The new rate is still being negotiated as of this writing in early 2008.

Unfortunately, many record companies don't like to obey the federal statute, so they amend it with the *controlled composition clause*. This clause means that for songwriters and composers whose copyrights are controlled by the company and any associated publishers, the record company will only pay ten times three-quarters (75 percent) of the minimum statutory rate. That's sounds complicated, but it means you will not be paid more than 75 percent of the statutory royalties due you on any ten songs you've given to your record label or related publishers.

The controlled composition clause is a cost of doing business as a songwriter or composer that is very hard to remove. If you are considering a contract, you might consider having your lawyer trying to knock this out on the grounds of federal law – but your chances are not good.

Some people's chances are better than others. If you work in a field that tends to use longer songs or pieces of music – think jazz, concert, or any type of music heavy on ballads – you may be able to make a better argument about how much you are being cheated. If you are a musician of great standing, you may get your way. But even then it is unlikely.

If you are offering a song for an album and you aren't under contract to the particular company that is putting together the album, the controlled composition clause *does not apply to you.* You are entitled to the full minimum statutory rate for your short songs and to the long rate for your long songs.

Still, many record companies will ask that you submit to the controlled composition rate. If you have sufficient standing, you might be able to refuse without the risk of being dropped from the album. The company is not likely to change its total royalty payment; the extra squeeze simply will be applied to someone else.

If you are an artist-songwriter, prepare to be squeezed. If for whatever reason the company has to relax the controlled composition clause for someone else, the money above 75 percent of the statutory royalties on ten songs is going to come out of *your* mechanical royalties. You will bear that cost, not the company. This is a similar idea to the recoupment system previously mentioned, only it is worse, because it cuts into the only source of royalties an artist-songwriter is assured to see from a record release, and can cut so deep as to post *negative numbers!*

Here are some scenarios drawn from real life, each one more harmful to an artist-songwriter's royalty position under the controlled composition clause:

- If you write 12 songs for an album instead of 10, you are going to lose royalties on two songs. The record company will not pay you for the other two.

- If on a 12-song album you write six songs and a non-performing writer controlled by the company writes six, you are going to lose royalties because the company won't pay for more than ten songs. But your fellow songwriter must be paid for all six songs. Therefore, you will only be paid for *four* songs. Any time a non-performing writer contributes songs that push the total above 10 songs, your royalties will be reduced in favor of the other writer being paid in full.

- If on a 10-song album some co-writer successfully insists on getting the full statutory rate, your mechanical rate will be reduced on all your songs to pay the difference.

- If the amount of royalties being paid to co-writers not covered by the controlled composition clause outside is *exactly* the maximum total royalties the record company is willing to pay, you could receive no mechanical royalties at all. You could sell a million albums under this scenario and never see a dime of mechanical royalties.

- If the amount of royalties being paid to co-writers not covered by the controlled composition clause *exceeds* the maximum total royalties the record company is willing to pay, you will *owe* the record company the mechanical royalties it has to pay out to your co-writers. In that case, the more albums that sell, the deeper in debt you will be!

If you are an artist-songwriter, you will have to be very vigilant about who writes with you for an album and how much they are entitled to, because the controlled composition clause is going to be next to impossible to knock out in your case, and will hurt you the most. Needless to say, if you are an artist-songwriter, you can't afford to make enemies among artists or songwriters. You are going to need their help and their graciousness in order to make any money.

The Work-For-Hire Clause

If you are ever told that you are getting a standard recording contract and it includes what's called a "work-for-hire" clause, *run*.

Generally, writers that work for companies that put out stock tunes are employed under "work-for-hire" clauses. The intellectual property they create passes directly to the companies for which they work – *forever*. The company is named as composer/lyricist; the only compensations the writers receive are paychecks or commissions.

Good "work-for-hire" jobs still exist – royalty-free libraries and designers for video games, educational software, and Web applications still make use of small but catchy melodies and riffs. The world of advertising does not use what were once called "jingles" as much as it used to, but there is still money to be made in that field as well. These are good "day jobs," and even decent careers. But a record contract is not supposed to be a work-for-hire arrangement.

You will need a lawyer with experience and understanding of the laws and practices of the music industry to get you through your contracts. You'll also need wisdom and courage like you've never had before in your career, because you're going to have to determine what you're going to fight for and what you can live with in terms of the fearsome problems the standard contracts present. You may also have come to a decision to walk away from a contract that is just too exploitative.

But if you walk away, then what? What about the distribution outlets you'll miss, and the advances you need to survive while devoting yourself to your craft? How will you gain access to fans old and new – and pay for your tours? How will you pay for venues and videos and merchandise and get it out to people? How will you achieve your dreams?

The *Freedom Guide* would not be worth the paper – or computer screen – it is written on if it did not have good answers for these questions.

To this point we have learned about fundamental things you'll need to do to get started on the business side of your art; now it's time to prepare for big change, first in your thinking about business and money, and then in your thinking about where you're going to find the cash and collaborative opportunities to do what you love. You might want to tighten the straps on your thinking cap, because the *Freedom Guide* from here on is going to take you on a wild ride.

Chapter 5: Why the Record Companies are Rich and You're Not, Part 2

You now may be thinking that there are a lot of powerful people in the music industry that are out to get you. If you pay attention to the news and to the conversation of your friends, you probably know that many people in all sorts of fields feel taken advantage of by big business. If you are a student of history, you know that workers over the centuries have been abused. So, the difficulties that you face belong in a larger context, and the larger context is a correct understanding of the nature of business in the capitalist world.

The Freedom Guide is not going to revisit the usual economic arguments. Forget Adam Smith, who is credited with being the father of capitalism, AND Karl Marx, who is credited with being the father of communism. Neither man talks clearly and honestly about the problems of modern business, problems that were already old when Marx and Smith picked up their pens.

Getting Paid for Your Work Has Been Hard for Centuries

It seems that the big problem with modern business is that it is very, very hard for the folks that do the work to get paid a decent wage. But perhaps you have never connected that fact to some history you may have learned in school. In Chapter 3 we talked about the Middle Ages and about people that had to work the land of nobles and kings in order to stay on that land – in a sense, people worked in exchange for their lives, not for a wage. This system was called *feudalism,* and the people who worked were called *serfs*. But at this time not much of what we think of as business existed.

Corporations and global commerce did not arrive until about the same time as colonialism and *chattel slavery.* Garrett Sutton in his book *Own Your Own Corporation* traces the rise of the corporation to the late 1500s. Wealthy European investors at that time got charters from their governments that would limit their legal liability in ventures they financed to exploit the resources of the New World; these charters were the basis for the first corporations. But the labor that produced the sugar, tobacco, cotton, coffee, rice, chocolate, gold, silver, and other raw materials that these wealthy investors traded, bought, sold, and converted to saleable goods in the early factories was often unpaid labor.

Every February you may hear in passing that African Americans living today are descendants of Africans taken from Africa and brought to North and South America as slaves. In February there is conversation about the millions of Africans kidnapped, packed tightly into slave ships and brought across the Atlantic. What is not often examined are some facts brought to light in Eric Williams' *Capitalism and Slavery:* the use of chattel slavery is what made agriculture in the Americas possible and profitable on a large scale. While "the [Native American] reservoir was limited," Mr. Williams writes, "the African [was] inexhaustible. Negroes were therefore stolen in Africa to work the lands stolen from the Indians in America." And work these Africans and their descendants did, unpaid, for centuries.

It should be noted that much, but not all, of the free labor done at the beginning of the modern world was done by Africans. Bartholeme de las Casas' 16th-century writings tell of the *encomienda* system that forced Native Americans into slavery in the silver mines of South America.

Just before African slaves were brought to North America, poor Europeans came to work under a system called *indentured servitude*. This system had chilling resemblances to the features of chattel slavery, as Philip S. Foner writes in his chapter of *African Americans in the U.S. Economy.* Foner reveals that for a period of time, kidnapping and packing into slave ships also befell European laborers. But more often, convicts and debtors were pressed into indenture, and conditions for indentured servants in the New World were often not much better than those for Africans in slavery. In *Nation of Nations*, James

West Davidson and his fellow authors point out that as many as 40 percent of indentured servants working in the Chesapeake Bay area in the 1620s did not survive the four to seven-year terms of work common at that time. Disease, malnutrition, and cruel treatment combined to kill off many poor laborers.

One might see from these brief historical examples that working hard, creating great wealth, but not being paid has been an equal opportunity problem for a long, long time. And yet somehow, business owners – the folks that owned the land grants in the Americas, owned the ships that moved goods and slaves and indentured servants back and forth, owned the patents and trademarks and copyrights, and owned the factories in Europe – made out pretty well in this same time period. The vast free labor pool available was very beneficial to these people.

Everything Old Is New Again

An unfortunate resemblance to the early history of capitalism and modern business can be found in the music industry today. The raw material in the music industry is the creativity of music creators and re-creators; the labor is the work musicians put in to create their songs or interpret other musicians' songs. The products are the publicly released albums, videos, etc. As we have seen, some music companies have found contractual ways to pay *no royalties, no recompense* to the musicians who create the incredible profit in the music industry. The major difference is that so many musicians keep offering themselves up to work for free because they don't understand how to protect and defend themselves and their work. The tendencies of big business may not change; it is up to musicians to prepare to meet the conditions.

History provides one frightening parallel example to the way musicians are treated by many music companies today, a parallel example that still existed on a considerable scale into the 1950s and 1960s in the United States.

Chattel slavery of Africans was eventually abolished, first in Europe, and then in the United States after the Civil War. But the plantation owners of the southern United States were not about to give up their free labor just because slavery had been declared illegal. They came up with the *sharecropping* system, which persisted so long that at least two generations of former African American sharecroppers – these are Baby Boomers and their parents -- are still with us.

In his portion of *African Americans in the U.S. Economy*, James B. Stewart notes the legal and institutional barriers African Americans faced in going in large numbers into industry, or even from working for themselves for decades after the end of slavery and Reconstruction. So, many had to return to work for their former masters after the Civil War. These African American laborers were to be compensated in this way: they would work the land, and receive as payment a share of the crops – hence the term, "sharecropping." This was the theory; reality for many sharecroppers was quite different.

In their portion of *African Americans in the U.S. Economy*, Daniel Fusfeld and Timothy Bates describe how many sharecroppers had to either purchase or lease their seed and equipment, in addition to the slave quarters they had once been housed in, from the plantation owners. But many African Americans had been prevented from learning how to read and write during the centuries of their enslavement. Thus, many had no way to defend themselves against terms in the leases and contracts they received that permitted the plantation owners to charge outrageous interest on the things they loaned. Nor did the sharecroppers have any right to look into whatever the plantation owners reported their debts were. Nor could the sharecroppers examine the reports on how big the crop had been, and whether they had actually raised enough crops to pay off their debt and turn a profit. Some plantation owners routinely said their workers still owed them at the end of the year. And so the sharecroppers had no choice but to *borrow* more seed, more equipment, take more bad contracts, and get deeper into manufactured debt, year after year, generation after generation. Slavery, by law, ended in 1865; debt bondage for many African Americans had not ended completely in 1965.

Do you see a parallel between this history and what you have been reading about in earlier chapters of *The Freedom Guide?*

The music industry's policy of recouping all costs for an album's creation makes every bit of what companies provide to musicians a *loan*; a loan constructed in terms so that it cannot be paid back in many cases. And audit clauses, without which you will never know if you have paid back the company's loan, are still hard to get.

Of course, the twist for the artist-songwriter comes from the controlled composition clause; no matter how much profit an artist-songwriter creates for the big companies, he or she can still owe more and more with each album sale. So, while musicians go deeper and deeper into manufactured debt, many music companies get richer and richer, year after year, business cycle after business cycle.

But there is hope. *The Freedom Guide* is not named as it is in vain. Musicians of all backgrounds and interests are finding ways around offering themselves up as ignorant victims to the big music companies. Just by reading this book, you are helping yourself avoid becoming another source of "free labor" to enrich the many music business owners who would like to exploit you. Take the time to understand what has been presented here, and then keep reading – more help is ahead!

Chapter 6: First, Free Your Mind

As I have already said, the key facts about the history of business, capitalism, sharecropping, slavery, and genocide in the Americas are public knowledge, though not often examined. You now know more about the world you live in, and what you are up against, than most of your peers in any industry. What you know is ugly stuff – but without the gloom, the gleams of hope would not seem so bright.

Business people outside the field of music have come up with good strategies for dealing with the realities of business and money. And here I draw out and give credit to Robert Kiyosaki, author of a series of books on money, investing, business, and even philanthropy, a series headed by the best-selling *Rich Dad, Poor Dad.*

An in-depth discussion of Mr. Kiyosaki's works is not possible in this book, but there are three observable laws of business and money he highlights that are key to your finding a way you can live with and be proud of in the music business:

- The rich invent money, while everyone else works for money (from *Rich Dad, Poor Dad*)

- The more people you serve, the richer you will become – and already are, though the money might not be around just yet (from *Rich Dad's Guide to Investing*)

- The most important action a business owner ever takes is to give the money and resources he or she has created back to the communities that have been key to that creation (from *Rich Dad's Guide to Investing*)

In my opinion, Mr. Kiyosaki deeply challenges much of the common thinking about business in that third point. For you as a music creator and re-creator, that third point translates to you at least giving proper credit to the people and communities that created or influenced the music you work with – we will take that up in detail in the Appendix. But consider this: the music industry's refusal to share fairly the profits of music sales with music creators and re-creators is damaging the whole industry, as artists find other ways to get their music to their fans, and fans find ways to get music and support artists without buying CDs.

For now we will take Mr. Kiyosaki's first two points; both are easily seen in the real world. Earlier in *The Freedom Guide* we learned how the idea – an immaterial reality – precedes the material reality of anything made by man. This is very similar to what Mr. Kiyosaki says about the rich inventing money in *Rich Dad, Poor Dad*; Mr. Kiyosaki points out that money starts as somebody's idea.

Specifically, rich people invent assets that produce money, an asset under Mr. Kiyosaki's definition being anything that puts money in your pocket. This book you are reading is a good example of an asset; it started as an idea, became a book, and is now generating money for me. You did pay for this book, right? But at the same time it can become an asset for you, since you will be able to use this to better your chances of earning money with your music. How this book becomes an asset for you depends on how your mind sees ways to use it – as Mr. Kiyosaki often hints, your mind is the real asset, from which your other assets, and your money, will come – or not.

Mr. Kiyosaki's point about becoming richer as you serve others is also easy to observe as an operating law of business. Fast food companies and the music industry serve millions and millions of people every day; notice how rich they are?

This also clarifies your own path as a musician; provided you are creating music that balances your self-expression with the needs of music lovers (or a niche of music lovers) and can get this music to them, you will be able to earn what you need to survive and thrive. In other words, you will be using your assets to invent money and resources for yourself by meeting the needs of others!

But nobody said this was going to be easy.

If you pick up Mr. Kiyosaki's books, you will find he went broke a few times on his way to writing his best-selling series. It took him a good while and a lot of failures to take his intellectual property – a book, as contrasted with your music – and get it to where it could serve others and make him very wealthy. You may expect similar struggles, but in the remainder of *The Freedom Guide* you will learn of resources that could make your way easier.

What I want you to take away from this section is that the money and resources you need to follow your calling are as limitless as your ability to perceive and your willingness to use them. This book is going to share *some* of the possibilities with you; it's up to you to go out and thrive with them!

Chapter 7: How to Find Millions, Millions and Millions . . .

Millions of opportunities and good ideas, at least, are passing you every day in this business of music. *The Freedom Guide* is going to alert you to only a small number of them, because you need to be able to pick up this book without breaking your arm. But the things you will learn about here will give you the tools to go out and find your own millions of opportunities.

Let's begin with a time-honored practice that has sustained musicians for countless ages before the computer was invented. This is the No. 1 way to find opportunities as a musician, now and forever, so pay attention:

Meet the Needs of Your Community with Your Music

There are elementary and middle schools that don't have art or music in them any more (get that fan base early!). There are senior centers that are packed with people who would appreciate hearing something beautiful. There are community colleges that have music departments that would welcome you into their classes and schedule you to perform with and for your fellow students, and would hire you to work with those music professionals also known as professors. There are festivals and fairs in many areas that need family-friendly entertainment. There are religious and other community centers that have people of all ages that would enjoy your music. And all these people, young and old, know people who know people who know other people . . . word can spread fast when people's hearts are touched.

Now some readers may be thinking that they don't want to write or play music that doesn't express them, their tight group of friends, or folks born in the same decade. To this I respond, *grow up*. Some of the best music deals with universal truths and experiences that resonate with all ages.

I am not saying try to please *everybody* with your total output of music; I am saying you should have some well-crafted works that you can play anywhere at any time that your entire community can love. If you love and serve your community, it will love you back; if you ignore your community, it will ignore you as well in your time of need.

Notice that I said "well-crafted works." While your community will support you and listen as you are developing your songs and your craft, the people who listen also want to hear your finest music, and they want it presented well. And when you engage yourself with community projects, those people expect you to fully invest your time, energy, and attention. This is their just compensation for supporting you when you are struggling. If you forget this compensation, you're sunk, because a community that feels used swiftly will turn its wrath on you.

Working within a community also requires a kind of wisdom expressed to me some years ago by a colleague I respect and admire: "I've been doing this long enough to know that if you don't go with the flow, you won't get anywhere." Community work is not for control freaks; most often you will have to work generously and patiently within the framework of others' plans.

Also, there is always more work to be done than can be paid for. If you limit your activities to what you expect to be paid for, you will lose priceless experience, good will, learning, and chances to make a difference for good, along with some excellent meals and a world of in-kind assistance that will never be for sale. So don't miss out; learn to serve your community.

The *Musician's Atlas*

If I stopped after talking about the *Musician's Atlas*, you would not be hurt much. The *Atlas* was the single finest directory of music resources and opportunities I had ever seen in print; it is now the finest strictly online directory I have ever seen.

In the *Atlas* (http://musiciansatlas.com/default.aspx)you will find addresses and contact information for clubs; college, land-based and Internet radio venues in the United States and Canada; festivals; song competitions and album projects; radio promotion; music press organizations; lawyers; conferences; regional promoters; publishers, associations; record retail stores – it goes on and on and on! Inside you will find every category broken down state by state and in alphabetical order, with each listing in the directory showing the right contact people, the kinds of music wanted, online and offline means of contact, deadlines – everything you need to know to decide the listed opportunity is for you.

Best of all, many of the dozens of entries in the "Conferences & Festivals" and "Contests, Compilations and Tours" are *free* for you to submit your music, online or off! There are at least 5,000 opportunities across the music industry listed for you, including the contact information of lawyers, promoters, agents, and managers to help you.

There is only one drawback to the *Atlas*, if you have a hard time staying focused, the *Atlas* can overwhelm you. Here's what I suggest:

- Get the *Atlas*, look at it, jump up and down and scream for joy at the hundreds of opportunities that appeal to you, celebrate your release from ever needing a record company or label again to get your music out, and then get away from your computer.

- Think carefully about what you have in time, energy, and music available, about opportunities in your area, and how much money you have to spend on promotion, agents, lawyers, etc.

- Go back to the *Atlas*; select ten things coming up in the near future that appeal to you and fit with what you can actually do.

- Research the ten opportunities and choose the best two or three, knowing that the next month will bring ten more opportunities into your reach.

If you present yourself professionally in enough places, your music and you will get wonderful exposure and ever-growing opportunities. But if you rush at everything at hand, you could sabotage yourself.

Remember, many people listed in the *Atlas* probably know each other (again, there are communities to reckon with), and they will talk to one another about what they find remarkably good or remarkably bad. If you make a fool of yourself by rushing submissions and presenting music and press kits that are not well done, the resources of the *Atlas* will close to you before you know it. Present yourself well, and the *Atlas* will be open to you for many years to come.

Access to the Atlas is not cheap; if you buy the monthly plan and let it renew every month, it will cost about $150 in a year – or, you can pay for a year at about $140 up front. But you DO have your thinking cap on, right? If you see that something is happening in the *Atlas* or other directory one year, you can always use the same contact information to find out if the people and organizations in the listing are doing similar projects in the *following year*. This also allows you to build relationships with the people and organizations you want to work with, and find out about opportunities not listed in anyone's directory. Now I am not saying you should not keep your subscription to the *Atlas* up to date -- given what it has to offer, the price is reasonable, every year. I am saying that you should think long-term, and, as always, save money when and how you can by paying attention, making good notes and files, and making the best first impression you can when you start making contacts. You can find out and do more with a month's subscription to the *Atlas* than most musicians will discover and do in a lifetime.

The American Composer's Forum

If the majority of your output is in European-style concert music, in jazz, or in electronic music and sound art, the *Musician's Atlas,* while still very useful, might not be quite as bottomless for you as it will be for your colleagues writing pop, rock, gospel, or blues. So to you I recommend joining the American Composers Forum, which is dedicated to "linking composers and communities," as it says on their Web site at www.composersforum.org. Here is the offline contact information:

American Composers Forum

332 Minnesota Street, Suite East 145

St. Paul, MN 55101-1300

Phone: 651.228.1407

Fax: 651.291.7978

The Forum offers a wide range of grants, readings, fellowships, commissioning and performing programs, and provides hundreds of links between its members and communities that want new music. The Forum has a long reach; it has about 1,700 members, including composers, performers, community centers, and educational institutions across the United States, with links to like-minded organizations across Europe.

Here are some of the Forum's additional programs:

- Innova Recordings, a not-for-profit record label to which any Forum member can send new music for consideration. Artists retain their copyrights, and records made by the label never go out of stock. Innova also has five Web radio outlets and puts up music on the label at iTunes, emusic.com and other Internet spots. The only trouble here is that none of this is cheap – the sample budget posted at www.innova.mu runs at about $5,000, and you have to foot that bill up front. So, you'll have to make some money elsewhere to do this – the other offerings of the Forum could help, and we'll talk about getting your music to make you some more money a little later. Or, you could collaborate with other musicians to raise the money. No matter what method you choose, there are no recoupment charges at Innova!

- Continental Harmony is a national commissioning effort supported by American Composers Forum, the National Endowment for the Arts, and several other foundations. As of this writing in early 2008, Continental Harmony has no calls for communities or composers, but what they do have is a wonderful "toolkit" that is worth reading if you are a musician deeply engaged with your community, or in a community group that is looking to work with such musicians. You can learn more at www.continentalharmony.org, or by calling Carey Nadeau at (651) 251-2814. Or e-mail harmony@composersforum.org.

On the Forum's main Web site and in the newsletter, there is something called "Opportunities," which is yet another excellent directory of chances for you to get your music exposure and perhaps garner some cash. These opportunities are listed by deadline date, and if you are a Forum member, you can log into the site to see detailed instructions for each opportunity.

Most of these opportunities are also listed in *Sounding Board*, the Forum's fine newsletter (it comes out six times yearly). The newsletter also features composers and performers talking about their successes, failures, and premiers (this is a huge source of ideas if you read with a careful eye) and also describes what programs and grants are currently available through the Forum for its members.

The cost of joining the Forum is $55 a year, or $100 for two years ($65 and $120 if you are outside the United States). Like the *Musician's Atlas*, the Forum can be well worth the cash. Still, like the *Atlas*, you need to have a plan before attacking the hundreds of opportunities available through the Forum, and before networking with its 1,700 members.

As you may have grasped from reading about Innova Recordings, the use of the Forum's resources is more expensive than those of the *Atlas*. Many of the competitions, festivals, and conferences you will learn about through the Forum have a fee attached for the submission of your music. You may not be able to afford fumbling around musical areas that are outside your skill set.

Here's another money-saving tip: Explore the Forum's Web site and see what it has to offer – you may not be at the right stage yet to make best use of its resources, and if so, you'll want to wait on joining. If you are at the right stage and don't have the cash, there is still one thing you can do. The "Opportunities" page won't let non-members see the detail of competitions and calls for scores, but it will show you the names of the organizations offering the calls for scores, composers, and proposals, and often the specific type of call.

Put that information into your favorite search engine, check for it in the *Atlas* or have your friendly telephone operator help you find phone numbers for organizations listed. Chances are, you can find a direct link to the organization offering the call, and thus get the detail you need without paying a dime. This can be time-consuming, but if you don't have the money to spare, it is a viable option. And, a fair number of the opportunities offered by the Forum are free to enter.

One more thing: if you are a student of the San Francisco Conservatory of Music or the New England Conservatory, you are already a member of the Forum by virtue of the conservatories' membership. Other students should check their schools' membership status as well, but any student in the United States can join the Forum at the reduced cost of $35 a year. International students can join for $45 a year.

Two Resources for the Christian Musician

If you are a writer of Christian contemporary music, the Christian Songwriting Organization and the Christian Songwriter's Network have tremendous resources and international networking opportunities. Two of the most successful international contacts I ever made came through my membership at CSO, and some of the best song critiquing I have ever gotten has been at CSO and CSN.

Both Web communities have articles on music and the music business from a Christian perspective, along with links to a startling host of resources, conferences, festivals, calls for songs, and potential album projects. Their Web forums bustle with conversation, collaboration, song critique, and opportunities to share your growing knowledge with your fellow Christians. CSO and CSN each have hundreds of members. Both are free to join. Or, just browse the sites, at www.christiansongwriting.org and www.christiansongwriter.com.

Don't Forget ASCAP, BMI, SESAC, and Others

Even if you are not a member of ASCAP or other professional music organizations, their Web sites have many hints and clues that you can investigate. Your local library has regional music publications that ALSO contain many hints and clues – check those with your local phone book and perhaps the *Musician's Atlas*, and you can access the information you need.

Welcome to a Wide-Open World

Can you see now that many opportunities in the music business are wide open to you? Can you handle the excitement?

But there may be a question: "How in the world am I going to get the money to go to all these festivals, enter all these competitions, make all those trips to the studio, prepare and mail all those press kits, and, and, and . . ."

Start with the low-cost or no-cost things you have learned about first, and work your way up – while you continue adding to your resume and your community connections. Be sure to keep people in your community informed of what your goals are; help could come from unexpected corners.

But there are also other ways that you and your music could make money that you probably aren't aware of – yet. Keep reading; *The Freedom Guide* isn't going to leave you without giving you tools to get what you need!

You also could find your way into "regular" stores, films, and radio stations at the same time.

Several online services offer free and inexpensive plans for you to have either your own freestanding webpage or Mp3 player to embed in Web sites or your MySpace, Facebook, or other social networking pages. Many of these services also allow you to sell your songs and to recruit affiliates to help you sell. I've run across a dozen or so companies like this, and here are my recommendations.

Nimbit

In the entire online world, Nimbit (www.nimbit.com) has the most complete set of services for the independent musician that I have ever seen. Their basic and free setup is as lavish as everything else they do – you get a live store page, to which you can upload all your artwork and Mp3s. You also get a catalog to put your works in, a blog, and an e-mail list to help you keep track of your fans.

You also can sell your Mp3s ($.49 minimum); Nimbit turns over 80 percent of the profit to you. You also can sell e-tickets to your concerts and gigs from your free site – rarely will a free service provide you this privilege. Nimbit offers not only pages for you, but an embeddable player as well to put in any site of your choice, and to give to your fans who want to help you sell.

Nimbit's paid options could cover a chapter all their own, but they include custom pages, promotional posters, print services for CDs and DVDs, and the set up of a merchandise store for you. At its retail level, Nimbit allows users to sell any physical product relating to their music directly to users, to submit songs to digital distribution outlets including iTunes and Rhapsody, and to send CDs to their partner site CDFreedom (http://cdfreedom.com) for additional sales. At the pro level, Nimbit adds several custom web design options, including MySpace customization, 8-page starter sites, premium templates, custom design, and hosting. You can check it out for yourself at www.nimbit.com.

Broadjam

Compared to Nimbit, Broadjam (www.broadjam.com) is a little scaled back in what it offers members on a free level – you can upload and sell Mp3s at 80 percent profit, and you get a free profile page, songlists, and fan pages. But the great strength of Broadjam, on any level, is Broadjam's access to ongoing contests, top reviewers, and uses of music – film, radio, and television -- in the entertainment industry.

I personally entered and semifinaled in the United Kingdom Songwriting Contest last year through Broadjam, and I found the process of submitting songs easy and highly streamlined. All Broadjam members receive discounts and benefits on entry and deliveries, with the discounts and benefits getting bigger as you upgrade your membership.

Broadjam offers three paid options in comparison to Nimbit's two. Broadjam offers greater Web options at each higher level, and Web hosting of your own domain at the Primo MoB level. Although Broadjam does not have an embeddable player, its paid options do allow video uploads and separate pages for photos, videos, albums, and contests.

Soundclick

The free offerings at Soundclick (www.soundclick.com) are about halfway between the functionality of Nimbit and Broadjam. You can upload videos, photos, and build your own "radio" station of songs by other Soundclick members (there are about 3 million at last count) in addition to uploading and selling your own Mp3s. A band page, message boards, free logos, mailing lists, and blogs also are included in the free option. You can also post news about your live events.

Soundclick also has charts to show how much your music is being listened to, which can be very helpful in determining if your song has popular appeal. Plus, it's just a boost – which I've had – to see your songs hit near or at the top of the charts!

For Soundclick there is only one paid level, called VIP. As with the two other services, you have much greater control over Web design at Soundclick's paid level. You can embed links to your songs and pages in other Web pages. This allows your fans to assist you in promoting and selling your work in a manner similar to what is possible with Nimbit. Also you are eligible for featured band rotation on Soundclick's home page. Soundclick also has advanced page and song statistics for its VIP members. But the best thing about the VIP option is this: there are no popups on your pages, and no ads shoving your page placement off-center, unlike with the free option! You can check it all out at www.soundclick.com.

Think Before Tackling the Three

If you think you are ready to hit the big time *for real*, Nimbit and Broadjam's free options will serve you well and the paid options even better. Between the two, all the ground that record companies cover – promotion, distribution, and sales worldwide – is covered very, very well. But you might not want to tackle either one unless your music is sparkling and your Internet business plans are finely honed. Nimbit and Broadjam can overwhelm the unprepared user. You can waste a lot of time and money trying things you are not ready for at both sites.

If you are new to setting up online music operations, if your music is not quite on a professional level, or if you're not sure in what direction you want to expand your promotion, distribution, and sales, you would be well served to start with Soundclick. Soundclick can carry you a long way if you know what you are doing – the networking opportunities implied in the building of your own Mp3 station are priceless, and free.

But if you have consolidated your fan base, figured out your niche markets, honed your music, perfected your means of getting traffic to your site, built your business team and are ready to interact with the larger commercial interests in the music world, Nimbit and Broadjam are ready for you.

More Options to Get Your Music Moving

Nimbit, Broadjam, and Soundclick are some of the big movers in the online music store world, but there are some other excellent options to choose from as well, options which capitalize on the mobility of embeddable players. There are not as many as there were when the first edition of the *Freedom Guide* came out. I give you one of the savvy survivors:

Soundloud

The greatest difference between Soundloud (www.soundloud.com) and its competitors is this: Soundloud will let you withdraw any money you make *daily*, with no minimum balance required. Soundloud's player also handles credit card transactions very smoothly, along with PayPal, Google Checkout, and Amazon payments. In no place might it be easier to pay and be paid than with Soundloud, and the secure checkout options will also be pleasing to your fans. Soundloud also offers a version for managers and labels to manage multiple artists within the same store. Check this out at www.soundloud.com.

How About Running Your Own Radio Station?

When you manage to get your online stores, your team of fans, your chosen method of getting traffic to your sites, and your business team in good working order, you might be ready to run something even bigger.   What we're about to discuss is a big step up from Soundclick's self-run Mp3 stations; what we're about to discuss will take in all your knowledge of performance rights organizations and licensing, the wonders of advertising online and offline, the skills of selecting good music to offer to the public, and just about everything else.   It's time to talk about the UnderGround Connection Network (www.ugcnetwork.net) – potentially your personal online radio station.

The UnderGround Connection

215-881-3506

P.O. Box 501

Wilmington, DE 19802

admin@ugcnetwork.net

You can build yourself into your own playlist, no matter what kind of music you write. You can also lease airtime for other people's shows on your station. You can stream live events from concert venues, churches, clubs -- anywhere -- on your station. You can release your albums and other folks' albums on the Network.

The Network is also in the process of going Internet television, which means users will have access to both radio and broadcasting.

The folks at the Network help you build your station and sell your airtime to advertisers; they will walk you through all the processes. They firmly believe that the success of the Network depends on the success of every member, so you won't get left in the cold with your new station.

The main thing you'll need is what the folks at the Network call the three D's – Desire, Drive, and Determination. But the fourth thing you'll need is $250 per month to pay for the streaming audio, the licensing fees, and the promotion the Network will provide to get listeners to your station. You also will have to sign up for at least six months, and that's $1,500. Still, if you work collaboratively with other musicians, you can afford this. Consider going to your community associates and *contracting* with them to sell them commercial airtime, to lease them time to hold a show or two every week, or stream their release parties and concerts on the World Wide Web, or release their albums with their commentary, and more.

Back in Chapter 5, we talked about Mr. Robert Kiyosaki; one of the other ideas he puts forward about business advancement is the importance of *cooperative thinking*, as opposed to competitive thinking. The Network is based upon the idea of community cooperation; there is no reason why you cannot access its resources by working cooperatively with the help of your fellow music creators and re-creators. If you can find a way to share the cost of *anything* suggested in *The Freedom Guide* by working out in-kind benefits with your associates, it will help you and those around you. As we learned from Mr. Kiyosaki in Chapter 5, the more people you serve, the richer you will become!

Still More Options to Get Your Music Moving

The sites I am about to list now are some of the biggest platforms for getting music directly to fans (if you are a composer/songwriter, now is the time to make sure you are working closely with the performers who are using your music); they are for you if are SURE that you are ready to hit the big time (as are Broadjam and Nimbit, actually). As I discuss these last online spots, bear in mind: you can only have ONE contract between yourself and retail outlets. In other words, if you are working through Nimbit to reach retail outlets, you can't simultaneously utilize any of the following services to access retail. So, consider what you want to accomplish and how, and choose wisely!

CDBaby

Just about everyone has heard of CDBaby (http://www.cdbaby.com); they have become the largest online seller of independent music. As of late 2010, CDBaby has paid out more than $25 million directly to musicians in sales for CDs and digital downloads. Musicians who have music on CDBaby tend to speak well of it; they have an excellent reputation for paying on time, every time, every week. CD Baby also gives its users access to retail outlets including Apple iTunes, Tower Records, Best Buy, Yahoo Music, Rhapsody, and more, in addition to sales at cdbaby.com.

CDBaby charges a one-time sign-up fee per album ($35) and per single ($9); after that, you can either manufacture your own CDs and artwork and ship them to CDBaby, or turn over the duplication of those items to CDBaby (for a reasonable price, of course). CDBaby takes a cut of $4 per CD and nine percent on all digital downloads – but since you can set your own pricing, the lion's share of the profit still comes to you.

Audiolife

Audiolife (http://www.audiolife.com) specializes in artist-to-fan direct transactions, and is serving some 100,000 artists worldwide. Audiolife's area of specialty might be said to be in getting artists' songs and merchandise everywhere and in every format a fan might want to purchase it, from traditional CDs all the way to app store-ready formats. Its fulfillment services include the know-how to manufacture and move large amounts of physical recordings and merchandise quickly and efficiently, combined with a technology focus on getting music to customers that are using social networking and using phones and other handheld devices to access the Internet. This can be an very attractive format since so much of making money as a musician is akin to collecting streams of pennies -- Audiolife is set up to get you as many streams of pennies from as many corners and niches as is presently possible. By reputation, the people that work for Audiolife are also passionate about music and about serving the artists that make it: they have set up infrastructure for artist services that is unique in the industry.

Audiolife is also integrated with several other important services, including Topspin, ReverbNation, and AEG -- the combined suite of technological savvy and manufacture-and-move know-how available through Audiolife and its partners is mind-boggling. And it is available to you for no upfront cost -- signing up with Audiolife is free. Audiolife takes a flat cut of sales from all music and merchandise sold -- you don't pay them until you make some money.

ReverbNation

Like Audiolife, ReverbNation provides a free sign-up for a very powerful platform for both artists and industry professionals – only it is nine times bigger, hosting close to than a million artists. ReverbNation describes itself as "homebase," providing tools for artists to work seamlessly with social networking, blogs and homepages, combined with excellent real-time stats so artists can see what's working and what's not in their promotions, marketing, and distributions. I have recently spoke to a user who has told me that ReverbNation is also a useful platform for finding gigs – which means you can find opportunities regionally to get exposure, performances, and of course, a little cold hard cash. ReverbNation also specializes in digital distribution to major online retailers – wherever you want your music to be, ReverbNation can most likely get it there! And, ReverbNation offers trending royalty reports – real-time access to knowing what money your music has made, as opposed to getting a report every 45 days.

Bandcamp

Bandcamp (http://www.bandcamp.com) is similar to Audiolife in that it is focused on getting artists to connect and sell their music (but not merchandise!) directly to fans, but it has a different approach, focusing on making sure each artist has a very well-built artist page -- without annoying ads -- around which to place all merchandising and purchasing infrastructure. Bandcamp's strengths are the SEO work to keep pages at the top of the search engines (but don't call your album something like "Without You." No SEO specialist can help you if your chosen name is that generic and common), and also keeping pages streaming and downloading music no matter how many desperate fans there may be hitting the page at one time. A measure of Bandcamp's success -- on Bandcamp, fans tend to buy whole albums (a higher-revenue item, of course) at about four times the rate that they buy single tracks.

One of the keys to Bandcamp's success is full-track streaming of every track -- that is, fans can listen to every song on every album the moment they arrive on an artist's page. The purchasing process is streamlined and easy -- music is available in any format a fan might want, and payment can be accepted in currencies used worldwide. Bandcamp also has excellent statistics for you to track sales, what music is being listened to, and how much. With this data you can also make decisions on setting your own pricing for albums, and also offering discounts to fans -- Bandcamp supports both of these options.

Bandcamp has a free signup, and then takes a 15 percent cut of your revenue until you reach $5,000 in sales -- then Bandcamp's cut drops to 10 percent.

Topspin

Topspin (http://www.topspinmedia.com) is yet another direct-to-fan distribution platform, and like Audiolife, it handles both digital product and physical merchandise equally well (fulfillment of orders for digital merchandise is handled by Topspin's partners worldwide). Topspin specializes in five marketing areas: fan-to-fan viral marketing, marketing targeted to creating new fans, direct marketing to existing fans, flexible offers (combining physical and digital products at customized prices), and thorough data analytics to help users keep track of what's working and what could work even better.

Like Bandcamp, Topspin can offer fans the music they want in all formats; they specialize in lossless formats and even HD video. But, if you are in the mood to add PDFs, Flash movies, collectible vinyls, screen savers, and a tote bag to hold it all, Topspin can also handle that. Topspin also immediately downloads a digital version of all music ordered in physical form, thus offering fans instant and long-term satisfaction.

Like Audiolife, Topspin's capabilities are mind-boggling -- both are true industry leaders in the direct-to-fan method of getting music out there, and both work with major labels and management firms because of the power and excellence and sheer volume of what they can do. Like Audiolife and Bandcamp, Topspin is affordable, but they have just changed their model to become so to the average musician. It used to be that you had to meet some very strict criteria to join Topspin. If you had a label or marketing deal, and your label or marketing service was affiliated with Topspin, you could join. If you were willing to sign up for a course at Berkleemusic.com -- "Online Music Marketing with Topspin" -- you would get a free Topspin account at the cost of your course tuition. If neither of those options worked for you, here are the four criteria Topspin used to require:

1. Do you make more than $5,000 annually selling music?
2. Do you have at least 2,500 emails in your email database?
3. Does your web site get at least 10,000 unique visitors per month?
4. Do you have at least 15,000 fans on Facebook?"

If you couldn't meet two of these four criteria, Topspin wouldn't accept you until very recently. I suggest you keep those criteria in mind. Topspin's old model was doing you a favor that no other service I have listed here was going to do for you -- until you have honed your music and built a fan base to start with (remember how I said to start in your community), NONE of these online services are going to do that work for you. If you don't know how to drive, it doesn't matter whether you are driving an affordable sedan, or a souped-up high-performance racing vehicle. You are still going to crash, because you don't know how to drive. The difference is the cost, in terms of survivability and replacement. Likewise in the music industry -- learn how to do your online marketing in the simpler, cheaper platforms first, and work your way up -- or not. Not everyone needs something like Topspin; Soundclick, used to its fullest (which will take time and study on your part), can do a great deal for you free or cheap.

One More Thing about this Online Setup . . .

I keep reading the stories of broken-hearted musicians online, and I don't want you to become one of them. So, consider yourself warned by someone who cares: if you put all your eggs in the basket of making money selling digital tracks or albums online, you are likely to end up broken-hearted and broke. I won't even get into the whole argument about the morality/legality of unauthorized copying and file sharing -- if you've read Chapter 2, you know my position, and I'm not going to waste your valuable time taking you through it again. You can cry on my shoulder if you want, but when you're ready to move on, you're going to have plan to sell other things (merchandise and licenses, for starters) with your digital downloads.

Go back and read again what the higher-end services I've listed here allow you to do. They are higher-end because they help you build multiple streams of income around your digitized music, streams of income that are based on physical products that CANNOT be copied a billion times and sent around the world faster than you can say, "Can anyone get the name of the jet that just carried away all my income?" Again, signing up with an online service is not going to help you if you haven't already thought out what physical product you want to move, and if you have thought this bit out well, you may not need a high-end partner (at least at first) to help you carry it out.

I'd start by offering a CD with gorgeous album art with it and on it – tell your fans it's a collector's item, and price it accordingly. If you've done your work and built a loyal fan base, those CDs will sell. Bandcamp comes to mind as a good choice for this approach, as they sell more albums than tracks on average. Then move on; past the t-shirts, mugs, and posters, you can put out lyric books, thoughts about the album/project from all the artists and composers involved, favorite fan comments and responses, "blooper" rehearsal videos – whatever your mind suggests a fan might be willing to pay a little extra to have their very own copy of. Again, these things can't be instantly copied – and if you take the time to PERSONALIZE something physical for a fan, you really have something that can't be copied and sent to a billion places.

On the flip side of this, a license (remember the chapters on copyright and royalties?) is also something that can't be copied and sent around the world; every person that wants to include your song in their project needs a license from you. You may have heard of B2B, or business-to-business transactions: I humbly propose that you might consider orienting your songs for M2M -- musician-to-musician -- licensing.

Can you position yourself to have songs ready for important events that are coming up, songs that other musicians might be happy to distinguish themselves by singing? Can you "personalize" songs for a particular local music group of regional importance, so that you can have your performing rights agency (your remember ASCAP and the like from Chapter 6, right?) pick up a little check for you from every venue? Can you collect some of your hottest beats from your hottest songs and offer them as a library to other local artists looking for samples? Can you network with local visual and performance artists and authors to see if your music or your lyrics might be just the thing for a narration, a background, a quotation? All these are situations in which you can collect licensing fees, and these fees are pretty much immune to the horde of "copy-and-send-and-never-pay" users who abound in online digital music transactions.

If you are diplomatic, you can sometimes write your own ticket in the world of licensing. Mechanical licenses, those that allow users to cover your song and distribute copies of it on CD or as digital downloads, are compulsory after a song's first use -- ever afterwards, you have to grant the license, and the licensees have to pay you 9.1 cents per song for short songs and 1.75 a minute for songs over five minutes (hence, the compulsion). So much for the compulsion; you can always ASK for more (and as a rule, my company, Praising Pilgrims Music, has always paid more than the going rate. Goodwill is priceless). In most other licensing situations beside the mechanical license, there is no pre-determined minimum amount. Everything is subject to negotiation. Don't be greedy, but do ask for what you feel is fair and diplomatically negotiate. Again, goodwill is priceless; if you get the reputation of being good and fair in the way you license your excellent music (before you try this, you will make sure everything people hear from you is excellent, right?), people may start to seek you out as a valued partner to work with!

Now about All of this Social Networking . . .

Changing gears here: I don't know enough about the different social networking sites to be able to compare them in terms of what is best for you as a musician. I can tell you one thing: there are thousands of musicians running after the latest social networking solution to the problem of getting exposure, fans, and money. And, I gather from looking at quite a few such setups that many of these thousands are doing little more than drowning each other out. Again, if you don't know how to drive, the vehicle doesn't matter -- MySpace, Twitter, Facebook, LinkedIn, and none of the rest can help you unless you've honed your music and know how to build a fan base.

Remember what I have said about meeting the needs of your community?

Take this into your social networking outlook. Instead of thinking, "How can I get these people to buy my music/merchandise?" think about, "How can I use what I have to meet the needs of my friends/followers/contacts?" Eric Byrnes, author of *Making Music Make Money,* refers to this as "relationship selling": when people believe they can trust you because you have consistently met their needs and met them well, they will be happy to help you keep doing what you are doing. And sometimes they will actually give you money for your offerings. But there is also something to be said for getting contacts, and building a network much, much bigger than you could ever build on your own BEFORE you even begin selling anything -- that is the power social networking gives you. In other words, Eric Byrnes' "relationship selling" goes on overdrive when combined with social networking, if you can discipline yourself to serve others first and reap the benefits a little later. But if you can't, there is a place for you among the thousands of artists and musicians that are drowning each other out -- but only there.

***

Now please do not launch yourself out in every direction at once – do some research, figure out what you want to accomplish, and start with the free options first.

But when it is time to pay for services, remember that back in Chapter 5, we talked about Mr. Robert Kiyosaki; one of the other ideas he puts forward about business advancement is the importance of *cooperative thinking,* as opposed to competitive thinking. If you can find a way to share the cost of *anything* suggested in *The Freedom Guide* by working out in-kind benefits with your associates, it will help you and those around you. As we learned from Mr. Kiyosaki in Chapter 5, the more people you serve, the richer you will become!

But before you run out and do all this, there are still a few more things you need to do to prepare yourself. Big advancement requires a big increase in knowledge, and the *Freedom Guide* has some ideas for you to continue your learning . . .

I hope that you will join me upon the continuous journey of learning about the business of the art that chose us – music – and of learning about the world in which we will make our music.

I'm going to share with you some of my favorite resources as a close to the main body of this book, and also some ideas and advice. Let's start with the books, some of which I've mentioned earlier, some of which I haven't. To save money, do what I've done – go to the library, or find a seat at a bookstore and expand your mind for free . . .

12 Great Books to Add to Your Knowledge

If you are a composer or songwriter, I suggest *Making Music Make Money*, by Eric Beall. Mr. Beall's book walks you – with a humorous twist that is welcome – through all the details of getting music from your desk through the Copyright Office, to music industry execs, past details of standard contracts, to the release party, into the record stores, into advertising, into films, and into putting money in your bank account. His is one of the few books written from the perspective of a songwriter and composer; his information on self-publishing and co-publishing is worth the cost of the book.

If you are a performing artist, I suggest *All You Need To Know About the Music Business*, by Donald S. Passman. Mr. Passman specializes in sharing how you go about picking your professional advisors – lawyers, accountants, managers, and the like. His book also contains much excellent detail on copyrights, royalties, and contracts.

If you would like to get a deeper understanding of the kinds of royalties your music can generate, there is no finer text than *Music, Money, and Success* by Jeffrey and Todd Brabec. This book is another one that you should take as several short courses; take the time to thoroughly understand each chapter before going on to the next one.

If you at some point decide to go into business for yourself as a musician, you'll need to learn more about money and business in general. I suggest you begin with *Rich Dad, Poor Dad,* by Robert Kiyosaki. Then move on to his *Cashflow Quadrant, Rich Dad's Guide to Investing,* and *Before You Quit Your Job.* Just the reading of his many trials and many, many errors has encouraged me through many a struggle. Mr. Kiyosaki learned from his mistakes, and in his books he passes on his knowledge – often quite hilariously – in a way anybody learning the ropes of business can understand.

Mr. Kiyosaki and his associates have also put out what is referred to as the Rich Dad Series, which covers every aspect of starting and running a successful business. All of these are excellent, but of them I suggest purchasing *Protecting Your No. 1 Asset: An Intellectual Property Handbook* by Michael A. Lechter, Esq. This will tell you more about intellectual property and how businesses are built around them.

An excellent companion to Mr. Lechter's book is *Own Your Own Corporation* by Garrett Sutton, Esq. Mr. Sutton's book walks you through the pros and cons of the different types of businesses – proprietorships, limited liability companies, and corporations – that you can build for yourself. If you ever start pulling in large amounts of money, or want to go into business with other people, Mr. Sutton's book could really come in handy.

If you really want to get into how modern businesses formed and settled certain habits, and Chapter 5 hasn't scared you off completely, I suggest *Black Labor, White Wealth* by Claud Anderson, Ed.D., and *African Americans in the U.S. Economy* by Cecelia Conrad, et al. The latter book contains the articles cited here on the roots of modern business and how the enslavement of Africans (which provided most of the free labor we were learning of earlier) was key to them.

If you are a student in college, university, conservatory, or even high school, I suggest *Campus CEO: A Student Entrepreneur's Guide to Launching a Multi-Million Dollar Business*, by Dr. Randal Pinkett. Dr. Pinkett's early claim to fame was winning *Apprentice 4*; Donald Trump loved what Dr. Pinkett came up with, and YOU will love it too. In fact, if you're not in school, and you read this book, you might want to go back. And that would not be a bad idea.

Study for Success in School

I suggest that if you have not taken some courses in business, you really should further your scholastic education. It wouldn't hurt you to learn about business taxes, bookkeeping, and marketing, and you should at least audit financial accounting, which will show you what makes businesses tick on a day to day basis. If you intend to run a business one day, you'll also want to take managerial accounting, which will help you cut down on trial and error when you put together your budgets for making, releasing, and marketing your music.

All the while you can take some music classes, meet the professionals who have "day jobs" as music professors, network with your fellow students, and harness the tools revealed to you in *Campus CEO* and in *The Freedom Guide*. The possibilities are endless.

***

I hope *The Freedom Guide for Music Creators* has given you the hope of freedom from ignorance and exploitation as you move forward with your musical career. More ideas await you in the Appendix, so we're not yet finished. But I hope you realize from this book that you have the power to protect and defend yourself from the dangers in the music business, and the power to find ways to reap monetary rewards from the publication of your music.

I thank you for allowing me to show you how to get to the possibilities of controlling your own musical destiny; what you do now is entirely up to you. My hope for you is that you will use your freedom and your music on the side of good always, and that you will discover the riches in meeting the needs of the people you encounter. I hope you make some serious money as well, and keep the wealth moving along to those in your community who are coming after you. Take care – and whatever you do, keep making music!

Appendix A: How to Make a Project into a Money Magnet

Yes, that's what I said.   This strategy could work across any genre, provided you are willing to put in a little research time, keep an open mind about genres you don't necessarily work with, and act in good taste and with proper gratitude.   And, if you are able to expand what you will learn here to its fullest, this chapter may be worth the entire book, to you and to your community.

Remember what you read in Chapter 2 about public domain music, and about how libraries across the world are stuffed with old editions of music upon which no one has copyright claims?   Please don't think, "There's a reason those libraries are stuffed with this music – nobody wants to hear that old stuff any more!" Consider three old folk tunes once known as "Aura Lee," "New Britain," and "Londonderry Air." You probably know these tunes better as "Love Me Tender," "Amazing Grace," and "Danny Boy."

Beautiful melodies (particularly if they are easy to sing) tend to last through the centuries.   Since humans have been loving, grieving, working, playing, worshipping, making war, making peace, living, and dying throughout history, good treatments of certain themes also withstand the test of time.

This brings me to the subject of niche markets. For a very simple example, the tune of "Danny Boy" is so lovely to so many people that if you can employ it recognizably, you will at least get people to listen at least for a while to your new words or take on it.   The niche market here, loosely speaking, is made up of people who love the tune of "Danny Boy."

People who love the tune of "Danny Boy" might love it as part of their devotion to folk music from Ireland, or the British Isles in general -- and people who love folk music from Ireland or the British Isles are two actual niche markets that are aggressively courted today.   Now while the folks in these two niche markets enjoy hearing "Danny Boy," they would be ecstatic to hear some contemporary of that tune that has fallen into undeserved obscurity. You could be a hero to these folks.

For another example, those who follow world music and those who follow the music of the Americas might have an interest in the incredibly diverse tribal music of both Africa and Native America, from which the majority of popular music has been derived for an entire century.

Here are some other big niches available for your immediate exploration; many old editions of European Classical music exist, and also most ragtime and early jazz and blues have passed into the public domain (quite a lot of this is available for free download right now at http://mutopiaproject.org). All these styles encompass instrumental, vocal, and choral selections – and, if you consider the Negro Spiritual, from which so much of blues, jazz, and popular music is derived, there are choral music selections roughly in the jazz/blues musical vein dating back into the public domain.

The Money Magnet

I have used the convention of the 10-song album throughout this book, and I'll bring it back one last time. Plan your projects out to hit a niche, or two, or three – but if you do multiple niches on a physical album, be sure they are related! Someone who likes folksongs from the British Isles may also enjoy the folk music of Colonial America, both from European settlers and African slaves. But it is less likely that someone who enjoys the classic blues is going to enjoy selections from the heart of Germany's Black Forest. So be careful when you choose types of music to include on your albums and projects.

When you have your album of tastefully arranged works ready, you will have something that potentially will be desirable to a sales base that includes one, two, or three niches, along with your loyal fans. If you play your cards right, you could even extend your fan base over your niche listeners and their communities – and that, of course, is the secret of the "money magnet."

But there are two big perils in this strategy, related to each other.

Be Careful With Your Arrangements

Notice that I said "tastefully arranged" when I referred to the arrangements on your theoretical cover album. Some songs lend themselves to freer uses than others.

Recently I heard George Gershwin's "Rhapsody in Blue" arranged as a 70s-style rock-funk piece, complete with wa-wa guitars. Think "Rhapsody in Blue" meets Jimi Hendrix and "Shaft," and you'll have the idea. I thought it was well done, with tremendous energy and humor. But I guarantee you that if I had heard the tune of "Sometimes I Feel Like a Motherless Child" or "Amazing Grace" treated the same way, I would not have had so favorable a reaction.

I am not saying to sacrifice what makes your sound special to your fans and supporters. I am saying you will need to strike a careful balance between old and new elements when you use works from the public domain.

Musicians in some genres may find this balance more easily than others. If you work primarily in the area of European Classical music, the amount of change you have to make concerns how to make a fresh but faithful interpretation of the works you find. By contrast, if you work primarily in the area of jazz, you are adept in the art of change, and can make gorgeousness out of any good thing you find. Many performers, composers, and arrangers work between these two signposts of stability and change, and a lot of world music has a stability of tradition that includes a great degree of improvisation.

The need to be sensitive to your audience(s) is never more critical than when you are working with public domain music; it is possible to cause fury in every niche market your cover album hits if you are not careful. If you find something you want to use for yourself in an area or genre of music with which you are completely unfamiliar, it would be wise for you to get together with musicians and community members who are familiar.

If you cannot achieve that, head for the other parts of the library and see if you can find some history on the peoples, the situations, and the needs and wants of the composer or communities from which your selected piece comes.

Give Credit Where Credit Is Due

Failure in this area will sink you, sooner or later. When you use public domain music, you must credit the composer and community from which that music came when you go public with your album or project. Let me repeat that: YOU MUST GIVE CREDIT.

Now, no law binds you to give proper credit to those that have no ability to enforce copyrights; hundreds of people have gotten away with the outright theft of other people's ideas before. On the other hand, there was once no civil law against evil child labor practices, or against the kidnapping and enslavement of folks from the continent of Africa. And some music companies still think it is just fine to rip off artists in the music industry.

Figure out what side of history you want to be on before you start using public domain music. Paul Robeson, the great African-American singer, actor, and thinker, said it so eloquently that I have also used it as this book's closing thought: "The artist must elect whether he will fight for Freedom or for Slavery." When you use public domain music, bear in mind that just the choice quoted is before you, though on a small scale.

As a purely business matter, the more composers' families and communities you enrage, the smaller your sales base will become – and you can't afford to shrink your sales base, because there is too much competition out there. You also will make enemies out of knowledgeable people who can help you on your way. Good opportunities will start to pass you by, because no one likes a thief but a bigger thief, who hopes to steal *with and from* the smaller thief.

On the flip side it can only help you to acknowledge where you find inspiration and material. You will become known as a person of gratitude and good taste, and your integrity will win you respect from many corners. Opportunities will flow from all such corners, opportunities you can be proud of exploring. And should the day come when someone tries to steal some music from you without giving you compensation or proper credit, you'll be doubly glad to know chickens aren't coming home to roost, and that your many, many allies from communities you honored are ready and willing to help you.

So, let's run through this again: when using public domain works, **YOU MUST GIVE CREDIT TO THE COMPOSER AND/OR COMMUNITY FROM WHICH THE MUSIC CAME. NO EXCEPTIONS.**

Appendix B: Selected International Copyright Offices

Canada

To access the online and traditional paper forms, go to http://www.cipo.ic.gc.ca, which is the website of the Canadian Intellectual Property Office. Go to the copyright section, and you'll get a choice of the e-form and the paper forms to print out.

Place du Portage I

50 Victoria St., Room C-114

Gatineau, Quebec K1A 0C9

1-866-997-1936

International calls: 819-934-0544

http://www.cipo.ic.gc.ca

Using fully online processes: $50

Paper forms: $65

Copyright protection in Canada lasts the lifetime of the author plus 50 years (with some specialized exceptions)

United Kingdom:

Concept House

Cardiff Road

Newport

South Wales NP10 8QQ

0300 300 2000

+44 (0) 1633 814000 (Outside UK)

http://www.information@ipo.gov.uk

The United Kingdom does not have a system of formal registration of copyright, but does encourage copyright holders to place a notice of copyright protection on their own works. Copyright protection in the United Kingdom lasts the lifetime of the author plus 70 years (with some specialized exceptions).

Australia:

Robert Garran Offices

National Circuit

Barton ACT 2600

(612) 6250 6313

(612) 6250 6666

http://www.ag.gov.au/cca

Australia does not have a system of formal registration of copyright, but does encourage copyright holders to place a notice of copyright protection on their own works. Copyright protection in Australia lasts the lifetime of the author plus 70 years, with one exception standing out from the rest: if a work is published after the death of the author, the effective copyright date is 70 years from the date of publication. That is, if an Australian composer died in 1850, and one of his or her works was only discovered and published this year, it would be protected until the year 2080.

India:

Dr. Suresh Chand

Dy. Registrar of Copyrights

Copyright Division.

Department of Higher Education

Ministry of Human Resource Development

4th Floor, Jeevan Deep Building

Parliament Street

New Delhi : 110001

Telephone No. : +91-11-23382436, (23382549, 23382458 Extn.: 31 & 45)

http://copyright.gov.in/

Fee for copyright registration of single work: 50 rupees.

Copyright protection in India lasts the lifetime of the author plus 60 years, with one exception standing out: very much like Australia, a work published after the death of an author has 60 years of copyright protection from the date of publication.

Still can't find the country you're in? Try the worldwide Directory of Intellectual Property Offices -- http://www.wipo.int/directory/en/urls.jsp!

"The artist must elect whether he will fight for Freedom or for Slavery. I have made my choice."

-- Paul Robeson

If You Have Found
This Book Informative...

If you have found this book informative and helpful to you as you handle your music business, we encourage you to buy multiple copies to give to the following:

- Family (because there are other musicians in the family, right)?
- Friends (because you have musician friends, right)?
- Fellow music students
- Musicians at your place of worship
- Community organizations that use music

All Praising Pilgrims Music books are available at special quantity discounts when purchased in bulk by corporations, organizations, churches, or groups. Special imprints and excerpts can be produced to meet your needs. For more information, call 650-204-1764 or write:

Special Sales

Praising Pilgrims Music Book Division

1432 Hayes Street

San Francisco, CA, 94117

Or: praisingpilgrims@yahoo.com RE: Special Sales

Or, if you are interested in a LICENSE and options for multiple, customized DIGITAL copies, please go to http://musicbusinessbasics.com/specialsales1.

Works Cited

Beall, E. (2004). *Making Music Make Money.* Boston: Berklee Press.

Cases, B. d. (1999). *Short Account of the Destruction of the Indies.* London: Penguin. Trans. Nigel Griffin.

Cecelia Conrad, et al. (2005). *African Americans in the U.S. Economy.* New York: Rowman and Littlefield Publishers, Inc.

James West Davidson, et al. (1990). *Nation of Nations.* Boston: Mcgraw-Hill.

Kiyosaki, R. (1998). *Rich Dad, Poor Dad.* New York: Warner Business Books.

Kiyosaki, R. (2000). *Rich Dad's Guide to Investing.* New York: Time-Warner Books.

Sutton, G. (2001). *Own Your Own Corporation.* New York : Warner Business Books.

Thall, P. (2002). *What They'll Never Tell You About the Music Business.* New York: Watson-Guptill Publications.

Williams, E. (1994). *Capitalism and Slavery.* Chapel Hill: University of North Carolina Press.

Glossary

Advance: Money a publisher or record company will give an artist, composer, or songwriter in advance of actual royalty payments – in effect, this is a loan against future royalties.

Audit clause: A clause in a contract that allows the artist, songwriters, and composers under contract to a particular publisher or record company to have the right to audit – that is, look at the books – of the company to see where the money coming in from royalties is being spent.

Controlled composition clause: This standard clause in a record contract provides that the company will not pay more than ten times 75 percent of the minimum statutory mechanical royalty (that is, 9.1 cents per song). Do a little math, and you'll realize that for many if not most of the albums in stores today, the record companies are paying only about 68 cents per copy to the composers and songwriters involved with the album.

Co-publishing: When a composer or songwriter shares the publishing duties (and thus, part of the publisher's share of any royalties) with his or her publisher.

Copyright: the right to make and distribute copies for works of music, literature, and visual art, and combinations of the same.

Copyright infringement: When someone makes a copy of someone else's work without getting permission from the copyright holder. In the world of intellectual property, we call it infringement; in the world of physical property, we call walking off with someone else's things *theft*. Essentially, the two terms are the same.

Cross-collateralization clause: A clause in a record contract allowing the record company to recoup, or retrieve the costs of making an album, from royalties not just from the album from which the costs came, but on all future albums and projects.

Public Domain: Music that either has passed the term of copyright protection (pre-1923 in the United States; 100 years is a good rule of thumb for the rest of the world) or has been placed in the public domain by the composer at the time of its creation.

Recoupment: This is the standard practice of record companies – they recoup all costs of an album from the album's royalties BEFORE paying the artist (but, composers, songwriters, and producers are paid from the first copy of the album sold).

Royalties: Payments made to copyright holders (the creator of the work and the publisher and record company when they are in play) for the use of their songs.

Sampling: Taking a bit of another song to make it a part of yours – most often riffs, beats, and breaks are sampled and looped and various ways to make up part of a track.

Self-publishing: When a composer or songwriter does all of his or her own publishing.

Sharecropping: In the United States context, this was a system under which landowners, mostly plantation owners in the South, provided living quarters, seed, and equipment for tenant farmers who would work the land. Landowners and farmers would share the crops and the profits equitably at harvest time – at least, in theory.

Work-For-Hire Clause: This clause in a contract provides that all work done by a composer or songwriter under contract belongs to the company, not to the composer or songwriter. This is common for companies that produce stock tunes and jingles, but should _never_ be in a standard recording or publishing contract.

CPSIA information can be obtained at www.ICGtesting.com
265597BV00001B/3/P